AWESOME NATURE

SPACE

AMICUS

sun

moon

Look for these words and pictures as you read.

spaceship

planet

Look at the night sky.
What is up there?

Space is all around us.

Stars are in space.

A star is a big ball of hot gas.

sun

Look at the bright sun.
The sun is also a star.
Its light keeps Earth warm.

moon

Look at the moon.
It shines at night in space.
Sunlight bounces off the moon.

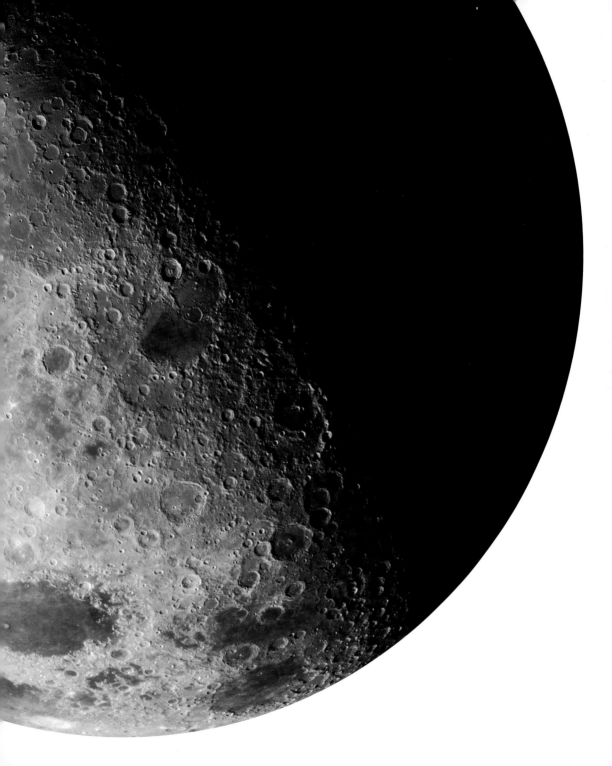

Look at the planet.
Our solar system has
eight planets.
Saturn has seven rings.

planet

Look at the spaceship.
People go to space
in a spaceship.
Blast off!

spaceship

Look at Earth.
This is how our planet
looks from space.

Look at the bright sun.
The sun is also a star.
Its light keeps Earth warm.

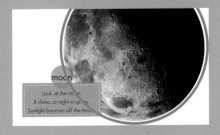
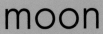

Look at the moon.
It shines at night in space.
Sunlight bounces off the moon.

sun

moon

Did you find?

spaceship

planet

Look at the spaceship.
People go to space
in a spaceship.
Blast off!

spaceship

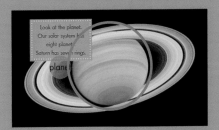

Look at the planet.
Our solar system has
eight planets.
Saturn has seven rings.

planet

Amicus Readers and Amicus Ink are imprints of Amicus
P.O. Box 1329, Mankato, MN 56002
www.amicuspublishing.us

Library of Congress Cataloging-in-Publication Data

Names: Kelley, K. C., author.
Title: Space / by K.C. Kelley.
Description: Mankato, MN : Amicus, [2018] | Series: Spot.
  Awesome nature | "Spot is an imprint of Amicus."
Identifiers: LCCN 2017022356 (print) | LCCN 2017034676
  (ebook) | ISBN 9781681513294 (pdf) | ISBN 9781681512891
  (library binding : alk. paper) | ISBN 9781681522494 (pbk.)
Subjects: LCSH: Outer space--Juvenile literature. | Readers
  (Primary) | Vocabulary. | Outer space--Juvenile literature.
Classification: LCC QB602 (ebook) | LCC QB602 .K45 2018
  (print) | DDC 523.1--dc23
LC record available at https://lccn.loc.gov/2017022356

Printed in China

HC 10 9 8 7 6 5 4 3 2 1
PB 10 9 8 7 6 5 4 3 2 1

Megan Peterson, editor
Deb Miner, series designer
Patty Kelley, book designer
Producer/Photo Research:
Shoreline Publishing Group LLC

Photos:
Cover: NASA/SDO.
Inside: Dreamstime.com:
Akiyoko74 2tl, Wikimedia 2tr,
Pere Sanz 3, Halil I. Inci 6.
NASA: 1, 2bl, 2br (JPL/NASA/
STSci), 8, 10, 12 (Carla Cioffi),
14. National Park Service: 4.

SPACE

2710